Look & Wonder

Myths
& Legends

Author

Jacqueline Morley studied English at Oxford University. She has taught English and History and has a special interest in the history of everyday life. She has written historical fiction and non-fiction for children including the prize-winning **An Egyptian Pyramid** in the *Inside Story* series. She is also the author of **Gods and Goddesses** in the *Look and Wonder* series.

Artists   Giovanni Caselli
                   Nick Hewetson
                   Pam Hewetson
                   Carolyn Scrace
                   David Stewart

Created, designed and produced by
THE SALARIYA BOOK COMPANY LTD
25 Marlborough Place, Brighton BN1 1UB

ISBN 0 7500 2740 1

Published in 1999 by Macdonald Young Books,
an imprint of Wayland Publishers Ltd
61 Western Road, Hove BN3 1JD

You can find Macdonald Young Books on the internet at: http://www.myb.co.uk

A CIP catalogue record for this book is available from the British Library.

Printed in Hong Kong.

Series creator

David Salariya was born in Dundee, Scotland, where he studied illustration and printmaking. He has illustrated a wide range of books on botanical, historical and mythological subjects. He has created many new series of books for publishers in the UK and overseas. In 1989 he set up The Salariya Book Company. He lives in Brighton with his wife, the illustrator Shirley Willis, and their son Jonathan.

Editor   Karen Barker Smith

Look & Wonder
Myths & Legends

Created and designed by

David Salariya

Written by

Jacqueline Morley

MACDONALD YOUNG BOOKS

Contents

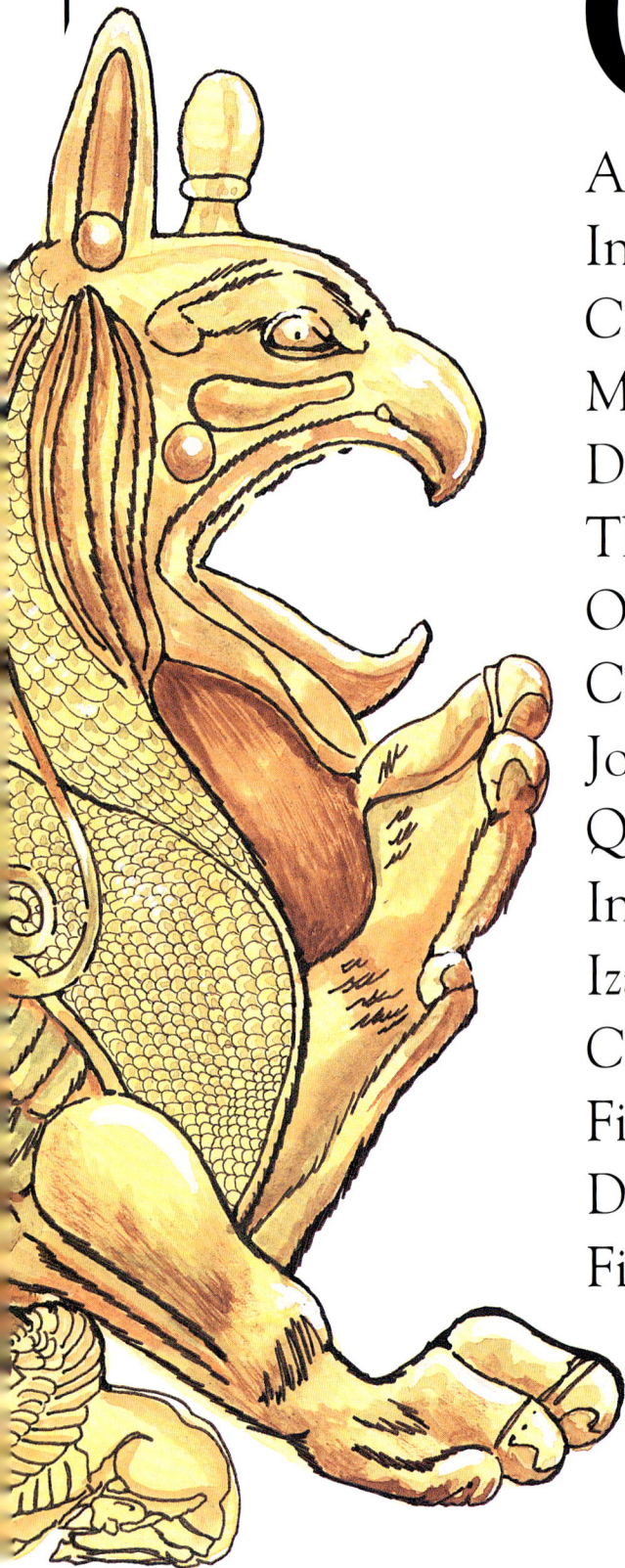

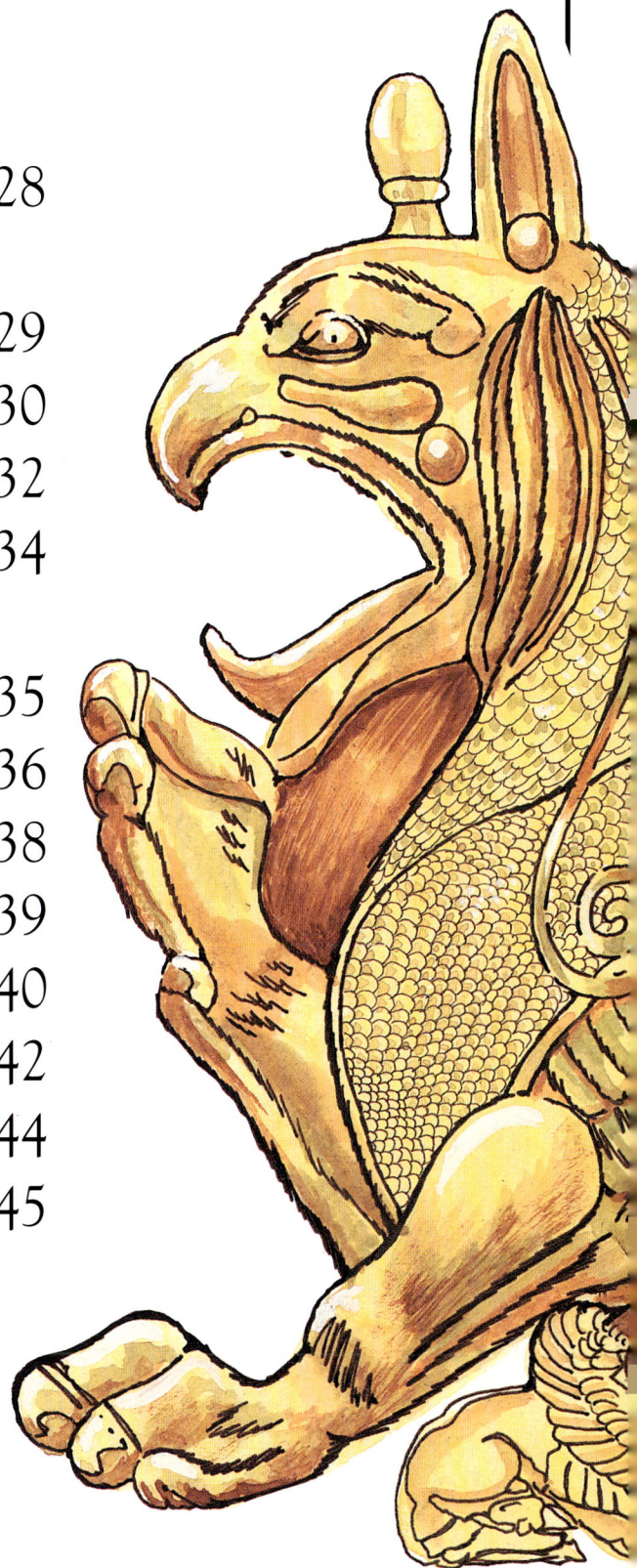

A world of myths and legends

This map shows the origins of a selection of the stories in this book.

1. Raven is a typical Native American 'trickster' hero, both mischievous and helpful, animal and human.

2. From the Nez Perce of the northwestern plateau of North America comes the tale of Beaver who brought people the gift of fire.

3. The New Mexican Zuni tell of a monster who ate the clouds.

4. The Aztecs of Mexico had a story about the King of the Dead.

5. The Urubu of the Amazon basin in Brazil know how the moon was made.

6. From Peru comes the tale of a llama who knew that a great flood was coming.

7. According to Irish legend, the Demon of the Lake was not as savage as he seemed at first.

8. King Arthur is the hero of a British legend which originates from Celtic traditions.

9. In the Norse mythology of northern Europe, Queen Hel ruled the underworld.

10. The unicorn was believed to actually exist and was a symbol of purity to medieval Christians across central and Eastern Europe.

11. The Minotaur of Crete is just one of the amazing monsters that appear in ancient Greek myths.

12. From ancient Mesopotamia comes the story of the she-monster Tiamat.

13. The ancient Egyptian god Osiris was killed and came to life again.

14. Anansi the spider man was so well loved that West Africans took his stories with them to the Caribbean.

15. The Nigerians have their own unique version of how the world was made.

16. Prince Rustam was a hero of Persian legend.

17. This fish is the Hindu god Vishnu in one of the many shapes he took to help the world.

18. From China comes the story of Yi, the Great Archer who saved the world from being burnt to a cinder.

19. When the Japanese goddess Izanami died, her husband tried to bring her back from the dead.

20. The native people of Australia tell countless stories of their Dreamtime.

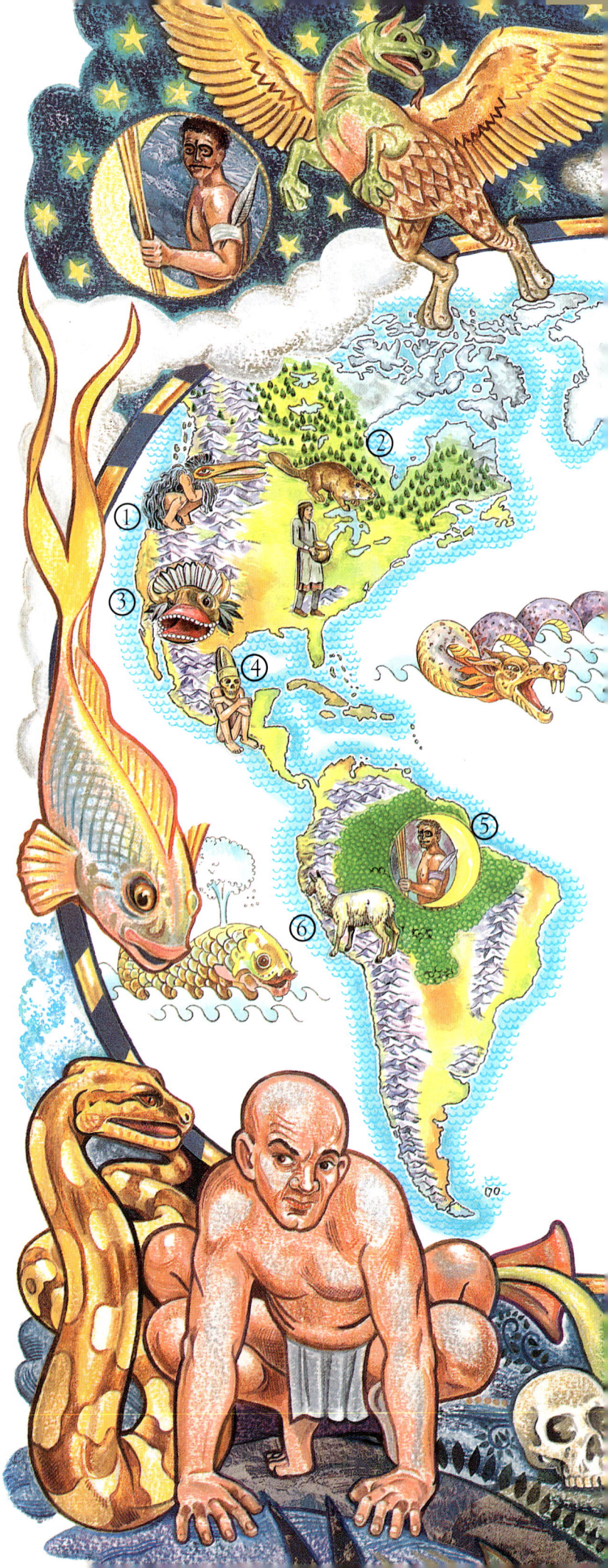

Introduction

The stories in this book are very old – so old that it is impossible to say who first created them. They come from all over the world and in their homelands these tales have been told and retold so many times it seems they have always existed. The stories often originated from people living much closer to nature than most of the world does now. Those early men and women – our ancestors – believed the Earth, the sun, the moon and stars were gods, or if they were not, gods had placed them in the sky. They asked themselves what sort of beings these gods could be, how they had made the world and why. How had the first men and women been created and what happened to people when they died? The answers to these questions took the shape of stories and were taught by one generation to the next. These ancient 'explanation' tales are called myths.

Myths tell of events that couldn't be explained any other way and tend to include supernatural beings – gods, goddesses and unearthly powers. The stories take place outside the normal, earthly concept of time and rarely refer to actual historical events. Legends are slightly different because they tell of 'long ago' – a time when monsters were common and heroes walked the Earth. Whether they are myths or legends, these stories are worth re-telling once again.

CHAPTER 1

Myths of creation

How did the world begin? Most mythologies tell that before anything else existed there was a 'first being' who made the world. With no world in which to set the story and only one character, often such myths do not have a lot to say about him (or her). It is when the first being creates other gods that things really begin to happen.

The ancient Egyptians believed that Ra the creator made Shu and Tefnut, the gods of air and moisture, and these in turn were the parents of Nut the sky and Geb the Earth. But Ra was in love with the sky goddess and was angry when he saw how closely the Earth embraced her. He ordered Shu to separate them for ever and that is why the air holds the sky high above the Earth.

The Maoris of New Zealand also say that the first two beings, Rangi and his wife Papa, hugged each other so tightly that when their sons were born they could not get out from between their parents. One of the sons began to push his father, Rangi, upwards with his feet. He pushed until he was upside down with the effort. His brothers helped him and together they forced their parents apart. Rangi became the sky and Papa the Earth. When the rain falls, Rangi is weeping with grief at his separation from Papa.

Shu holds up the body of his daughter Nut to form the arch of the sky so that she can no longer reach her beloved Geb. This picture (right), based on a painting more than 3,000 years old, shows how the ancient Egyptians imagined the scene.

Detail (above) from an intricately carved decoration in a Maori meeting-house. Rangi, the Sky Father, and Papa, the Earth Mother, the first parents of the Maori nation, are shown embracing each other.

Dreamtime and grapevine

The Aboriginal people of Australia believe that the world about them is the creation of their spirit ancestors. These ancestors sleep beneath the earth or in the rocks or trees. In a period called the Dreamtime, the ancestors awoke from their slumber and walked the Earth, some as humans, some as animals or plants. Wherever they went they touched the desert and the rocks and living things took shape beneath their touch. Here and there they found strange unformed lumps lying on the ground. They made knives of stone and carved these lumps into people, giving them faces, arms and legs. Wherever the spirit ancestors passed they left sacred signs upon the landscape, in the shape of a rock, a waterhole or a tree. Such signs are everywhere, for the Dreamtime and the spirit ancestors are never far away.

The Mandans of North America say that, in the beginning, their people lived in an underground world by the shores of a great lake. One day a group of their men were out hunting when they came across a mass of gnarled roots hanging down from somewhere far above their heads. They began to climb it. After a long climb they discovered at last that they had scaled the root of an enormous grapevine that was growing in the world above. This world was very pleasant. The sun was shining, the plants were tall and green and there were animals in every thicket just waiting for huntsmen. The men scrambled down the root and told their families of their wonderful find. The whole of the Mandan people decided to move to the world above. The tribe set off and began to climb the vine root. It swayed and creaked under their weight but was safe until a very heavy woman insisted on trying to climb up. Her weight broke the root and those who were waiting behind her had to remain in their underground world. The Mandans in the upper world did not forget their first home completely. Mandan people believe that after they die they will return there to live beside the lake.

The Mandans are one of the Sioux tribes of the Great Plains. This portrait of a Mandan chief (right), wearing a necklace of bear claws comes from a photograph from the 1890s. His name was Rushing War Eagle.

The first woman

After the world was made the gods created men and women. There are many different accounts of how this apparently happened. In many myths, it appears that the creator god felt the world lacked something until it had people in it. Gods or goddesses created human beings out of sticks, clay or by some magical means. Men and women were usually formed together, as companions, but there are several stories that say women were created later. The ancient Greek version of this story is unfair to women, suggesting that they are to blame for the troubles of the world.

Zeus, king of the gods, was not pleased with the new race of men that had appeared on Earth. He suspected the men – and one in particular named Prometheus – of plotting with his enemies the Titans and wanted revenge. He created a beautiful woman and sent her down to Earth. Her name was Pandora, meaning 'all gifts', for Zeus told the gods to bless her with every charm that would make men love her. Aphrodite, goddess of love, gave her beauty and Hermes, the gods' messenger, gave her wit and guile.

The moment Prometheus set eyes on Pandora he guessed that Zeus was up to something. He warned his simple-minded brother, Epimetheus, not to get involved with her. But Epimetheus was kind-hearted and took Pandora into his house. She had brought a box with her, a present from Zeus which he had told her she must never open. But Pandora soon grew bored and longed to look inside, though Epimetheus begged her not to. She waited until his back was turned and lifted the lid of the box. Immediately, a swarm of hideous creatures shot into the air: envy, sickness and old age, lies, treachery, famine and war. Pandora shrieked as they flew out into the world, where they have been tormenting people ever since. One tiny creature fluttered after them, and that was hope, the only comfort Zeus allowed humankind.

The Cherokee people of North America say the first woman was Selu the Corn Maiden. Selu gave birth to the first corn plants by rubbing her stomach. In this painting of the Green Corn Ceremony (below) Cherokee women representing Selu carry baskets containing the first crops of the year. Their corn is actually maize, the crop on which their lives depend.

Obatala's creation story

A Nigerian legend

In the beginning the great god Olorun ruled the sky. Below there was nothing but water, for the world had not yet been made. One day the young god Obatala peered down from the sky and thought how dull the water looked. "Something should be done to brighten it up," he thought. So he went to Olorun and asked permission to create land. "You may certainly make land," said Olorun, "if you know how."

Obatala consulted the magician god Orunmila. "You must first make a golden chain, as long as you can," he told him. Then you must fill a snail-shell with sand and put the shell in a bag, together with a white hen, a black cat and a palm nut. You must climb down the chain with them until you reach the water."

When Obatala had everything he needed, he took the bag, hooked the chain to the edge of the sky and climbed down. But the chain was not long enough and Obatala couldn't quite reach the water. "Use the sand in your snail-shell!" Orunmila called down from the sky. Obatala emptied the snail-shell into the water and the sand made a small dry hillock in the water. "Now free the white hen!" called Orunmila. Obatala dropped the hen onto the hillock where it immediately began to scratch and scatter sand to the left and to the right. Wherever the sand fell it formed land all around. Obatala dropped down from the chain, dug a hole and buried his palm nut. At once a palm tree shot up and dropped more nuts which grew into a shady forest on the land. Obatala made himself a house of palm bark and roofed it with palm leaves. There he lived, with just his cat for company.

Olorun looked down from the sky. "Is all well?" he asked. "Well enough," replied Obatala, "but it is not so bright here as in the sky." So Olorun tossed the sun down to shine on the world. Finally, Obatala made little figures out of clay and put them in the sun to dry. When Olorun breathed life into them they became the first men and women in the world.

CHAPTER 2

Journeys to the dead

Telepinus, the Hittite god of fruitfulness, rejected the world and vanished into the wilderness. Without him nothing grew and the gods tried everything to find him. Eventually he reappeared, riding on an eagle's back (below) and brought the world back to life.

Stories of corn gods are widespread. When corn gods die or disappear it has a negative affect on harvests. Like seeds that seem dead in the earth in winter, such gods are often believed to go underground. In their absence the earth is barren and nothing grows. But like the seeds of corn they generally spring back to life again.

Osiris was the corn god of the ancient Egyptians. Long ago, when the gods lived on Earth, Osiris ruled Egypt. He taught people to grow corn and vines and ruled them well. But his evil brother Set was jealous and murdered him, nailing his body into a chest and throwing it into the River Nile. The river carried the chest to the sea, where it was washed far away. Osiris' sorrowing wife Isis searched the world, until at last she found the chest magically encased in the trunk of a tamarisk tree. She brought it secretly back to Egypt. However, Set found its hiding place, hacked the body to pieces and scattered the bits along the Nile. So Isis built a boat of papyrus reeds and once again searched the waters until she had found each piece. Through magic, prayers and love, she breathed new life into her beloved Osiris.

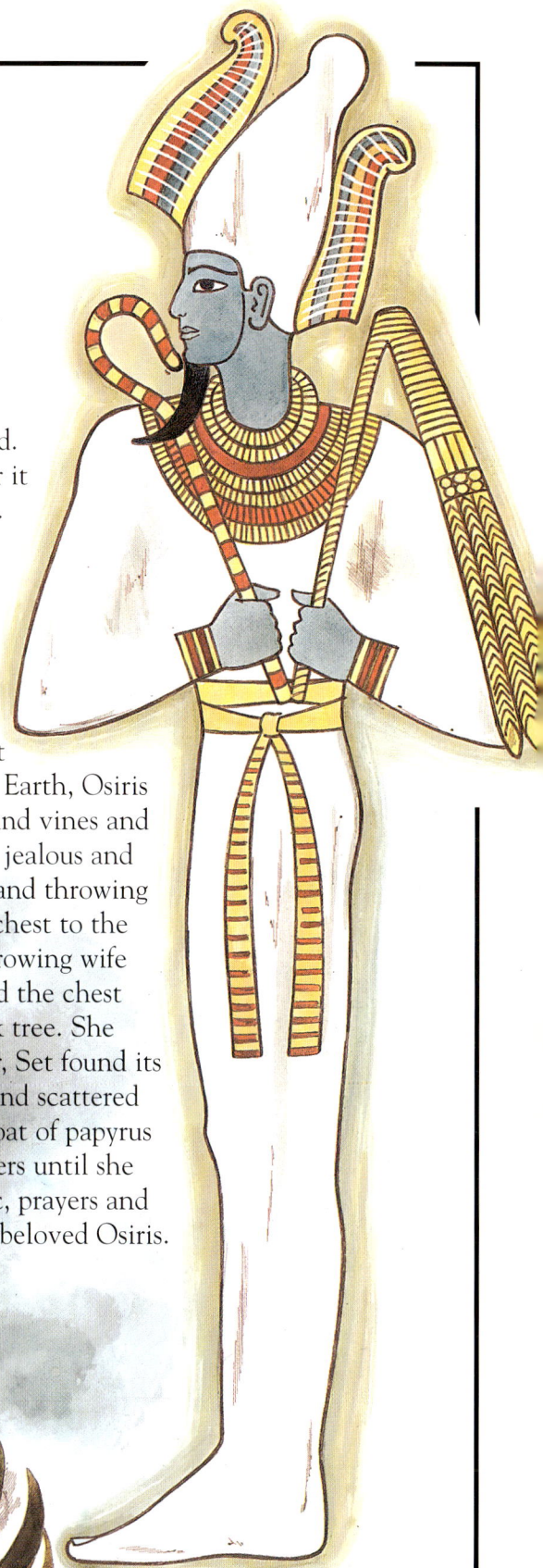

Osiris was always portrayed wrapped up like a mummy (above). This was not an image of death but a symbol of rebirth. Mummification preserved the body and this, the ancient Egyptians believed, enabled a person's soul to live after death, as Osiris had done.

Quest for a loved one

In the Norse story of Baldur the Beautiful, Baldur was the best of the gods: the wisest, the kindest and the most gentle. Everyone loved him, except Loki, an evil god who was the father of monsters. Baldur's mother Frigg made every stick, stone and living creature in the world swear never to harm him, but she forgot to ask the mistletoe plant. When Loki learned of this he used mistletoe to bring about Baldur's death. He made the plant into a dart and tricked the blind god Hodur into throwing it at Baldur. The gods were stunned by the death of Baldur. His brother, Hermod the Swift, rode to Niflheim, the Land of the Dead. He rode through dark valleys for nine days and nine nights until he reached its ruler, Queen Hel. Hermod knelt before the queen and begged her to let Baldur come back from the dead.

Queen Hel was the daughter of Loki. She was terrible to look at because one half of her face was beautiful and the other was cruel and wrinkled. She turned the fair side of her face to Hermod and agreed to make a bargain with the gods. If everything in the world above Niflheim was willing to weep for Baldur, he could return from the dead.

Hermod rode back to the gods in triumph – he did not doubt that every stick, every stone and every living thing would weep for Baldur the Beautiful. And so they did, all except one old woman who lived alone in a cave. "She is deaf," people said. "She has not heard about Baldur." They shouted at her to weep but she only glared at them. "My name is Dry Eyes," she replied, "and if you think I'll weep for Baldur you are mistaken. Let Hel keep him!" The old woman was Loki himself, who had taken another shape. As Loki had ruined Queen Hel's bargain, Baldur had to remain in the Land of the Dead.

The ancient Greek story of Orpheus also deals with death. Orpheus was a marvellous musician. No living thing could resist the enchantment of his lyre playing. He married the wood nymph Eurydice, but their happiness was short-lived – Eurydice died of a snake bite and left her husband broken-hearted.

In desperation he went into the underworld to plead with its ruler, King Hades. He stood before the king's throne and played his lyre. Hades was so moved by the music that he restored Eurydice to her husband with one condition: Orpheus must turn his back on her and not glance round until they reached the upper world. Eurydice cried out to Orpheus as she followed him, so that eventually he turned to her. She then faded into the darkness and was lost to him for ever.

In the underworld

Aeneas, the greatest hero of Roman legends, was summoned to the underworld by his dead father in a dream. Aeneas' journey to the underworld is one of many tales told about him in a long poem called the *Aeneid*. The poem describes how Aeneas had to flee his native city of Troy when the Greeks destroyed it. After many adventures the gods sent him to Italy, where his descendants founded Rome.

To learn how to reach the underworld Aeneas consulted the Sibyl, a priestess who uttered prophecies from a vast cavern in the mountains. "First," the Sibyl told him, "you must find a tree with a golden bough and break off the branch. Proserpina, Queen of the Underworld, will demand this gift."

Aeneas was guided to a tree by a pair of doves and returned with the golden bough. The Sibyl warned Aeneas of the danger and then led Aeneas deep into her cave. The Earth trembled and a passage to the underworld opened beneath their feet.

The Sibyl brought Aeneas to the banks of the dismal river Acheron, which circled the realm of Pluto, king of the dead. Aeneas saw a multitude of dead souls scrambling to board a ferry boat, while the ferryman, a grim old man called Charon, pushed many of them away.
"Why does he take some and not others?" Aeneas asked. "Only the properly buried may enter Pluto's kingdom." the Sibyl replied. "The unburied must wait a hundred years upon this shore."

At the sight of the golden bough Charon grudgingly took Aeneas and his companion across the river. There, Pluto's watchdog Cerberus howled at them with his three heads and bristled his snaky back. The Sibyl tossed the dog a drugged cake to silence him. She led Aeneas through fields of spirits, among whom he recognised dead comrades. He heard the bitter reproaches of his former love, the Queen of Carthage, who had been so in love with Aeneas that she had killed herself.

Before long the route divided. To the left was a flaming river and the fortress in which the evil deeds of the dead were punished. To the right the path led to the pleasant fields of Elysium where heroes, poets and philosophers strolled and talked. Here, Aeneas was at last greeted by his father, who told him of his future, foretelling his son's triumphs and the founding of Rome.

Quetzalcoatl, whose name means 'plumed serpent', was an Aztec god in ancient Mexico. He wore a crest of coloured feathers from the quetzal bird.

Quetzalcoatl decided to give the world a new race of human beings. He went down to Mictlan, the land of the dead, and found Mictlantecuhli, its lord, seated on a pile of bones. "Give me the bones of my father," Quetzalcoatl begged. "Whatever lies here is mine" was the answer. "What do you want with them?" "I need them to make the world a new race." said Quetzalcoatl.

Mictlantecuhli agreed to let the bones go if Quetzalcoatl could perform a task. He had to blow into a conch shell, making a great noise, while walking four times around a circle of jade. Quetzalcoatl blew with all his strength but no sound came, for the shell was blocked with earth. He asked the worms that lived among the dead to wriggle into the shell and clear it so it could produce a blast of sound. Mictlantecuhli gave Quetzalcoatl the bones, but told his servants to make sure he did not leave with them.

The servants covered a pit with branches so that Quetzalcoatl fell into the trap and lay senseless. Birds swooped on the scattered bones and pecked them to dust. When Quetzalcoatl recovered he scraped up the bone-dust as well as he could, moistened it with his own blood and moulded it into a new human race.

Izanami and Izanagi
A story from Japan

Izanami and Izanagi were children of the First Being, who existed before anything was made. They stood on the floating bridge of heaven and stirred the ocean with a jewelled spear. The drops that fell from the spear formed the first land, an island where Izanami and Izanagi then lived happily together. Izanami gave birth to the wind god, the moon god and the sun goddess. But when she gave birth to the fire god she was so badly burned that she died.

Izanagi travelled to Yomi, the Land of the Dead, to find his wife and bring her back. He heard her voice but could not see her in the darkness. "I have eaten the food of Yomi and cannot return with you," she told him. "Go back and do not look at me."

But Izanagi longed to see his wife. He broke off a tooth from the comb in his hair and set light to it to make a torch. What he saw made him rigid with horror. Izanami's body had begun to rot and maggots were crawling over her flesh. Izanami was bitterly ashamed to be seen in such a state. She cried out in fury and summoned the demons of Yomi to destroy her husband.

Izanagi fled, with the demons close behind. When Izanagi reached the entrance to the upper world he closed it behind him with a boulder which a thousand men could not move. From behind the boulder Izanami's voice screamed to him, "Every day I will cause 1,000 people to die and bring them to this land."

"And every day I will cause 1,500 to be born," Izanagi replied, and he returned to land of the living.

CHAPTER 3

Fire and flood

Earthquakes, volcanoes, and floods – disasters like these were thought to be caused by the gods.

According to a Chinese tale, the world had not been made very long when the god of water and the god of fire had a war and nearly ruined it. The god of water summoned all his underwater creatures and went into battle. But his forces could not withstand the fire-god's heat. It melted the jellyfish and roasted the rest of his army. The water god was so furious, he rammed his head against the mountain that held up the sky. The mountain split and fell, making deep gashes in the Earth. Lumps of the sky fell down and water gushed from the cracks in the ground creating an endless sea. It was up to the creator goddess Nu Wa to mend everything.

A flood that covers the world is a very common myth. Often, the people of the world are blamed, for displeasing the gods. In a Babylonian myth the gods sent a flood because people on Earth were irritating them by making too much noise. The Hebrew god, Yahweh, found the world had grown incredibly wicked. There was only one man in it worth saving – Noah. Before Yahweh flooded the world he told Noah to build an ark (a large ship) to house himself, his family and two of every living thing. After the rain stopped, Yahweh put a rainbow in the sky as a sign that he would never drown creation again.

After 150 days Noah thought the flood waters seemed to be receding. He released a dove from the ark to see if it could find dry land, but it found no place to settle and flew back to him. When he sent the bird out a week later, it returned with an olive twig in its beak. And so Noah knew that somewhere there must be trees showing above the water.

A flood destroyed the legendary city of Atlantis (right), so the ancient Greeks believed. It was said that a giant tidal wave swallowed the island. The sea god Poseidon had built the city and given it walls of brass and palaces of gold. The remains lay somewhere at the bottom of the ocean, but no one has ever found them.

Drowning the world

Matsya the fish – a Hindu myth

A holy man named Manu went each morning to pray by the river, pouring its water over his head from a water pot. One day he found he had scooped up a little fish in his pot.

"Don't put me back!" the fish pleaded.

"If you do, the big fish will swallow me."

So the holy man took the little fish home in his pot. The next day when he looked into the pot he found the fish had grown and could hardly turn round in it.

"Please, holy man, find me more room," it begged. So Manu filled a cauldron with water and put the fish in that, but still it grew and still it begged for more room. Next Manu dug a pond for the fish and tipped it in. The fish was enormous now and soon filled the pond. So Manu took it to the sea.

As the giant fish slipped into the waves it shone with dazzling brightness. Manu suddenly realised that it was no ordinary fish but the lord Vishnu himself, the Preserver of the Universe, and he bowed before it. Vishnu spoke to him from the water, "My name is Matsya the Fish. In a short time the ocean will rise and drown the universe and a new creation will appear. You must build a ship and fill it with all the plants and seeds, birds and beasts that are needed for this new life. All the while, pray to me and I will save you." Then the fish dived beneath the waves.

Manu built the ship as he had been told and every day he prayed to Matsya. Then the storm came. The sea flooded the land and Manu saw the fish swimming towards him. Its scales were of shining gold and it had a golden horn on its head. It told Manu to throw a rope around its horn and it towed the boat to safety through the waves, to a mountain peak above the waters. Vishnu saved that one holy man to be the father of a new race.

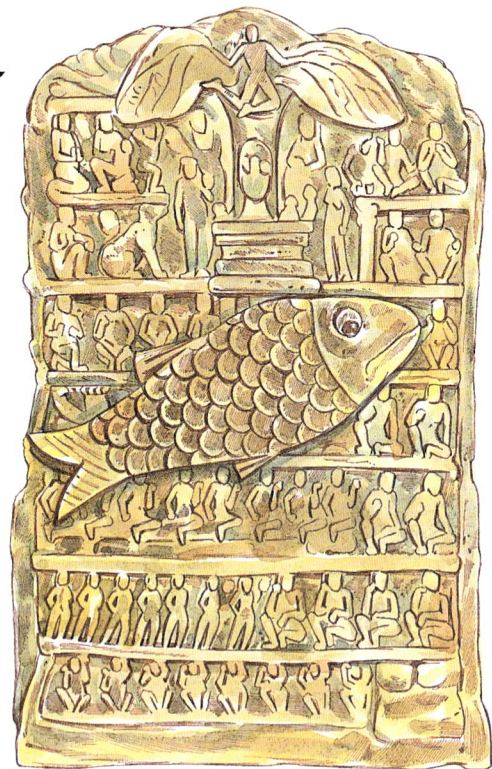

A relief showing Vishnu as Matsya (above). Vishnu came to Earth nine times to save humanity. Hindus believe his tenth appearance is yet to come.

A Peruvian myth tells of a villager and his llama. The villager led his llama to a mountain pasture where the grazing was good. But the llama would not touch the grass. It put back its ears and cried 'yu, yu', which llamas do when they are unhappy. The man was exasperated. "Why do you moan when I have climbed all this way to find you grass? Eat, you fool!" he yelled.

"Do you think I am sad without reason?" the llama replied. "Know that within five days the sea will rise and drown us all."

Discovering that his llama could speak, the man asked if it knew any way they could save themselves. "You must take food for five days and follow me to the top of Mount Villcacoto," replied the llama.

When they reached the mountain they found many birds and animals already gathered there. Soon, the sea rose and covered the land until only the tip of the mountain was above water. Some animals were hardly able to get a foothold on dry land. The fox could not keep his tail out of the water, which is why foxes now have a black tip to their tail. When the water retreated the only human being left alive was the man at the top of the mountain. Therefore everyone in the world is descended from him.

Fire from the gods

For early peoples, fire was a precious possession, providing them with warmth and light. But they knew that if they lost control of it, fire could destroy them. This could be the reason why so many ancient myths describe fire as a power belonging to the gods – humanity was perhaps never meant to have it. All over the world there are tales of how fire was stolen from the gods and given to the people of the Earth.

According to the ancient Greeks, Prometheus the Titan stole fire from heaven for humankind. He smuggled out a small, glowing ember. From this he lit a flaming torch and brought it down from the skies. Zeus punished him with eternal torment in the underworld.

The people of the Fiji Islands say that a terrible fire giant lived in a cavern in the hills. He had teeth of fire that shot out flames whenever he opened his mouth. The villagers were afraid to go near him, but they had no fire of their own. One night a group of bold men tiptoed into the cave while the giant slept and set fire to a bundle of twigs from his burning breath. The giant leapt up and chased them down the hillside into a small cave, but they blocked the door with a boulder. "I know you have my fire in there!" the giant raged. "Let me have a look."

The men rolled the boulder back a little way and the giant thrust his head in. Then they gave the boulder a mighty heave so that it split his neck against the rocks. The villagers had gained the power of fire and had no further reason to be afraid.

The Nez Perce people of North America say that long ago, before there were any people in the world, animals and trees walked and talked just as we do now. In those days the pine trees had the secret of fire. They would not share their secret with any being that was not a pine tree.

One winter, it was so cold that the animals almost froze to death. They called a meeting and decided that someone must steal fire from the pines.

Close to the Grande Ronde River, the pine trees built a great fire to keep themselves warm and they set guards all around to keep the animals away. But Beaver had hidden himself in the river bank and when a hot ember rolled down the bank he ran off with it. The pine trees chased him along the bank until he took to the water and swam across. By now the pine trees were getting tired so they stopped at the river bank. So many stopped there, and so close together, that even today people can hardly get through the trees at that spot. Only the Cedar tree went on chasing Beaver.

Cedar said, "I will run to the top of that hill and see how far ahead he is." Beaver was very far ahead, too far to catch. He gave fire to the willows, the birches and to many other trees. Ever since then these trees have shared the secret of fire. Cedar still stands on the top of a hill and there are no other trees anywhere near him because of how far he ran.

It is easy to see why early peoples believed fire lived in trees. If two pieces of wood are rubbed together in the right way the friction between them produces a spark.

This Native American (above) is using a piece of equipment called a fire stick to make fire.

The great archer
A Chinese legend

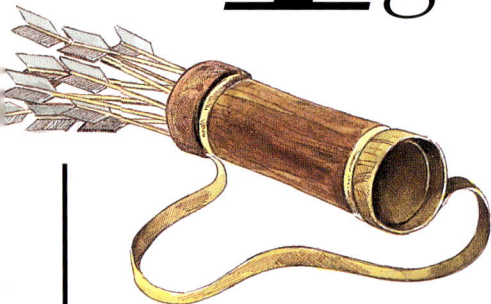

Long ago there was not just one sun but ten. These suns were the sons of Di Jun, the god of the East, and his wife, Xi He. Their home was in the boiling Eastern Sea where they lived on an enormous tree which towered into the air from the waters. Xi He only allowed one of her sons to ride across the sky each day. Before each dawn Xi He prepared a flying cart and brought it to the top of the tree. The sun of the day bathed in the boiling sea, got in the cart and drove it carefully across the sky, shining just enough to warm the world and make things grow. This duty became very boring and one night the ten suns decided they would put up with it no longer.

One morning, before their mother arrived, they all danced into the sky together. The world below felt the heat of all ten suns. The rivers and the seas dried up, the forests shrivelled and the fields caught fire. King Yao saw his people scorched and blinded and sent an urgent message to Xi He. But the ten suns laughed in the sky and would not obey their mother.

Eventually King Yao summoned Yi, the Great Archer. He gave him ten arrows and ordered him to shoot the suns out of the sky. Yi climbed a rock, took careful aim and brought one of the suns tumbling down. Its light went out and it fell to the ground as a dead crow. Two, three, four, five, six, seven crows fell and the heat lessened. As Yi prepared yet another arrow the king cried out. "Leave us one sun!" he called, but Yi was too far away to hear. He shot the eighth sun and the ninth, but as he felt behind him for the tenth arrow he found his quiver empty. King Yao had sent his swiftest runner over the rocks to snatch the last arrow. One sun was saved and that is the one that shines in the sky today.

CHAPTER 4

Heroes

A hero is someone who performs noble deeds and fights for good against evil. The heroes of myths were often related to the gods. Others were shadowy historical figures surrounded by amazing and fantastical legends. An ancient example of this kind of hero is Gilgamesh of Babylon.

The deeds of Gilgamesh are recorded in a vast poem which dates from c. 2000 BC. He was king of Uruk and was a strong but overbearing ruler. His subjects complained to the gods, who created a wild man called Enkidu to humble him. But after a fierce bout of wrestling, Gilgamesh and Enkidu became firm friends.

When Enkidu died, Gilgamesh was left broken-hearted and afraid of death. He decided to consult his ancestor Upnapishtim, whom the gods had made immortal, to learn how to escape death. To reach the dwelling of Upnapishtim, Gilgamesh entered the mountain where the sun goes down. Beyond the Sea of Death he came finally to his friend's home. At first, Upnapishtim gave him no hope. "All things must die," he said, "unless the gods will it otherwise." But Upnapishtim's wife persuaded him to reveal the secret of a plant that grew at the bottom of the ocean. This plant could make the old become young again. Gilgamesh set off and weighted his feet with stones to sink to the sea floor, where he found the miracle plant. But as he stopped to bathe on his way home a snake crept up and swallowed the plant. So Gilgamesh returned to Uruk sad and empty-handed.

Gilgamesh fights the Bull of Heaven (above). The goddess Ishtar sent it to ravage Gilgamesh's kingdom because he had enraged her by refusing her love. It was Enkidu who finally tore the bull to pieces, so Ishtar caused him to fall sick and die.

The legend of King Arthur (left), is loosely based on a historical figure, perhaps a Celtic British king who fought invaders in the 6th century. Arthur proved himself a true king by pulling the sword Excalibur from a rock. When his leadership of his Knights of the Round Table ended in betrayal and bloodshed, the king was wounded. A ghostly boat took him to the mystical island of Avalon where he remained for ever.

The labours of Heracles

The greatest hero of Greek legend was the champion Heracles. He was a favourite of the Romans too, but they called him Hercules. He was amazingly strong – when he was still in his cradle he strangled two serpents with his baby fists. These serpents were not there by chance but had been sent by Hera, queen of the gods, who did everything in her power to injure Heracles because she hated his mother.

When Heracles grew up, Hera set out to ruin him by sending him into a fit of madness in which he killed his wife and children. When his madness passed Heracles was in despair at what he had done. He went to the oracle at Delphi to ask what he must do to wipe away his guilt. He was told he must become the servant of his cousin, Eurystheus, and perform ten tasks that he would set him.

Eurystheus was Hera's favourite, a nasty, cowardly little man and he sent Heracles on the most dangerous errands possible. His first task was to kill a monstrous lion that was devouring the people of Nemea. Its skin could not be harmed by steel or fire so all weapons were useless against it. Heracles killed it with his bare hands and afterwards wore its skin as armour, with its gaping head as his helmet.

Heracles threw away his weapons and choked the Nemean lion to death (right). As no knife could pierce its hide he used one of the bear's own claws to skin it.

Heracles' next task was to kill the Hydra, a many-headed monster that lived in a swamp. When one head was cut off, two grew in its place. Heracles seared each severed throat with fire, so that new heads could not grow. But Eurystheus refused to count this labour among the ten because Heracles had been helped by his chariot driver lighting the fire.

Heracles' third task was to kill the ferocious Erymanthian boar. He presented the boar to Eurystheus who was so scared he hid in a jar and would not come out.

Eurystheus then sent Heracles to clean the stables of King Augeius, who had such vast herds of cattle that their dung piled up to people's knees. The King agreed to pay Heracles a tenth of the cattle if he cleared the mess, which he did by knocking down walls and diverting a couple of rivers through the stables. But Eurystheus would not count this labour either. He said Heracles had been employed by the King, not by him. King Augeius refused to honour his word too. He said the river god had done the work!

Because of his cousin's meanness Heracles did two extra labours, twelve in all. Zeus made him immortal as a reward and even Hera became his friend.

Trickster heroes

Heroes are usually admired due to their courage and glorious deeds. But there are quite different types of hero that crop up in stories from many parts of the world. They are the cunning 'trickster' heroes who always outwit their opponents and are often up to no good. They are heroes, certainly, because in the tales told about them they always win the day and come out on top. It seems that such trickster figures reflect the rebellious, cheeky side of human nature. In Native American myths, Raven is this type of hero: unpredictable and selfish but sometimes a friend to human beings. Below, a story is retold from the Tinglit and Haida peoples of the North Pacific coast about Raven. He brought people light by tricking the great sky chief out of his most prized possession, the sun.

The Polynesian hero, Maui of a Thousand Tricks, thought the days were too short so he caught the sun in a noose and gave it a beating. Since then it has only been able to limp slowly across the sky, making the days much longer.

Raven turned himself into a pine-needle and dropped into the stream where the sky chief's daughter was drinking. By swallowing the needle she became pregnant and eventually gave birth to a baby boy, who was Raven in disguise. The baby became a favourite with his grandfather, the sky chief, who let him play with anything he wanted. One day Raven pointed to the box in which the sun was hidden. First his grandfather shut the smoke hole in the roof of the lodge. Then he opened the box.

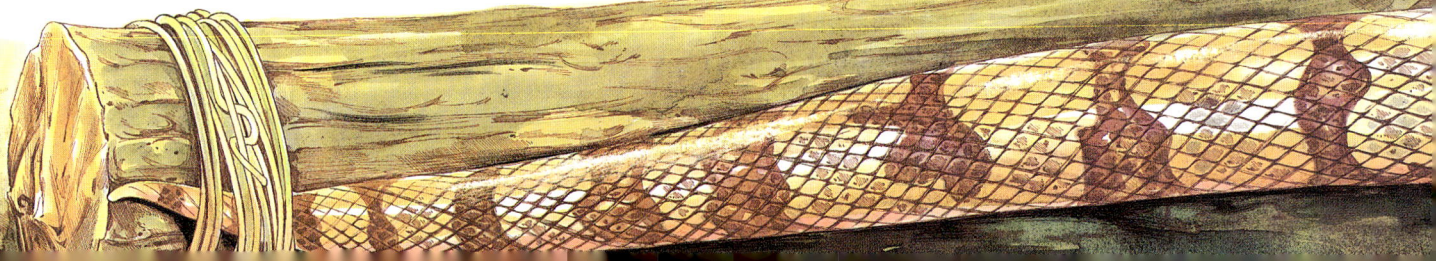

Below, a Kwakiutl (North Pacific Coast) dancer wears a ritual mask. He is enacting the role of Raven in a religious ceremony.

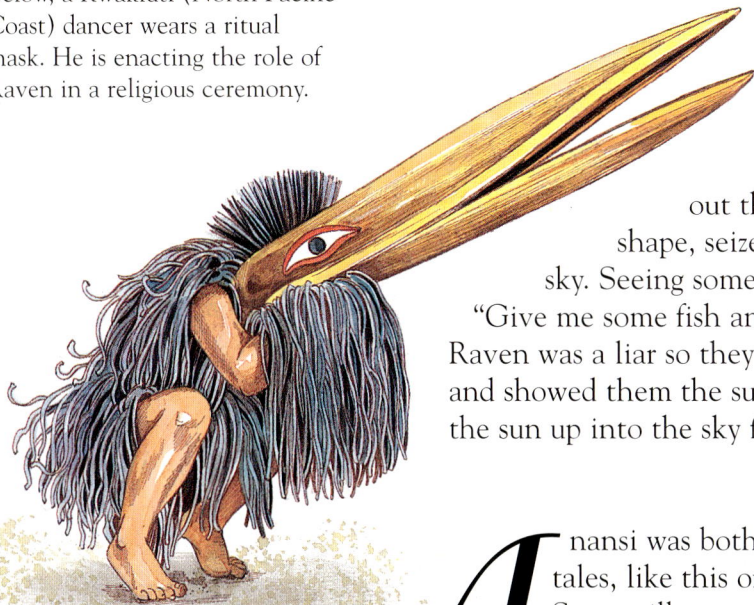

At once the lodge was flooded with light. The baby rolled the fiery ball of the sun round the floor of the lodge until he seemed bored with it. The sky chief let him have it whenever he asked but always tucked it back in its box afterwards.

One day the chief was feeling drowsy and forgot to close the smoke hole when he took out the sun. Raven changed back into his bird shape, seized the sun and flew through the hole into the sky. Seeing some fishermen by the river below he called out "Give me some fish and I will give you light." The fishermen knew Raven was a liar so they laughed at him, but when he lifted his wing and showed them the sun they gave him their fish. Then Raven threw the sun up into the sky for everyone to enjoy.

Anansi was both a spider and a man and is the hero of many tales, like this one from West Africa and the Caribbean. Some villagers were in despair about a giant python that was preying on their children and animals. They went to God to beg for advice. "You had better ask Anansi to help you." said God. "He is always boasting how wise he is. If he can't get rid of the python I shall punish him for boasting. But if he can, I will grant him even greater wisdom." Anansi took a dish of mashed yams, palm oil and eggs and put it near the python's hole. When the python came out to eat, Anansi spoke to it politely and admired its length. "You must be as long as the trunk of that tree over there."

"Longer," smirked the python.

"Let's measure you," said Anansi. He cut the tree down with his axe and the python laid itself alongside. He was not quite as long as its trunk. "If I lash your tail to one end and you give a good pull, I'm sure you can stretch the extra bit," said Anansi. The python let himself be tied at the bottom and, while he was concentrating on stretching, Anansi tied him at the top as well. He then chopped the snake into pieces.

Anansi boasted so much about his triumph that God hurled a pot of wisdom at him. It hit Anansi in the middle and nearly split him in two, which is why all spiders have such narrow waists.

The demon of the lake

There was once a lord of Ulster named Briccriu of the Poisoned Tongue. He held a feast to which he invited King Conor of Ulster and all his heroes of the Red Branch. He also invited the bravest of them all, Cuchulain, the Hound of Ulster. After a while, Briccriu provoked a quarrel amongst them as to who was the greatest champion of all Ireland. It was agreed that the choice was between Cuchulain, Conall of the Victories and Laery the Triumphant.

"The only creature fit to judge between them is the Demon of the Lake," Briccriu declared, so the demon was summoned from the water. The demon strode into the hall carrying a huge axe which he offered to the three contestants and proposed a test of courage.

"Any one of you may cut off my head today," he said, "but the same one must let me have a stroke at his neck tomorrow."

Conall and Laery withdrew from the test, but Cuchulain took the axe and struck the demon's head from its body. The demon picked up his bleeding head, took his axe and returned to the lake. Next day he reappeared, quite whole again, to claim his half of the bargain. Cuchulain knelt and put his head on the block, trying to hide his fear. The demon swung the axe in the air and brought the blade down... onto the wood of the block. He told Cuchulain to rise, the bravest champion of all Ireland.

CHAPTER 5

Monsters: good and evil

Cerberus, the monstrous watchdog of the ancient Greek underworld, appears on this dish (below). He warned of the arrival of new souls and prevented the dead escaping.

A monster is a creature unknown in the natural world, often an amazing being made up of various parts – the head(s) of one beast, the body of another – parts that nature never intended to go together. In the world of myths and legends monsters appear everywhere: the Anglo-Saxon hero Beowulf fought Grendel, a bloodthirsty water-monster; the native North Americans dread Windigo, the ice-monster that devours solitary hunters; in Fiji, people fear the Ngendei, a being that is half snake, half rock.

Not all monsters are bad. One of the most appealing monsters is the unicorn. The ancient Greeks and Romans believed there really were such animals. In the Middle Ages the unicorn was a symbol of purity. It was believed that unicorns were extremely wild and could only be tamed by a pure young girl. Legend has it that when a unicorn dipped its horn to drink, the water, no matter how foul, was purified. This showed that unicorn horn could make poisonous substances harmless. Their horns were in great demand, even up to the 17th century, for checking the food of kings and nobles who feared plots against their lives. Most of the 'unicorn' horn used had actually begun life as part of a narwhal, a small member of the whale family with a long, spiralling tusk.

Greeks and Romans described the unicorn as an antelope or wild ass with a long, sharp horn on its forehead. It was reported to live in India (a belief probably started by sightings of rhinoceroses). By medieval times unicorns were usually portrayed as horses with long, twisted horns.

Monsters of the classical world

Ancient Greek legends are full of monsters. Killing one was the regular way for a hero to show his worth. The hero Theseus was not much more than a boy when he faced one of the most savage, the Minotaur. His father, the king of Athens, had to send seven maidens and seven boys to the island of Crete to be fed to this bull-headed monster. When he heard this, Theseus insisted on being one of them. The king of Crete himself thought it a pity to sacrifice such a princely young man and offered to let him be fed to the Minotaur last of all. Theseus refused this, but was helped instead by the king's daughter, Ariadne, who had fallen in love with him. She gave him a ball of thread and told him how to use it to find his way through the maze in which the Minotaur lived. In return he vowed to marry her. However, after killing the monster and escaping the maze, Theseus abandoned Ariadne on an island. According to legend, the wine god Dionysus found her and carried her off to the sky.

Cyclops were giants with a single eye in the middle of their forehead. The hero Odysseus and his men were imprisoned by the Cyclops Polyphemus in his cave, but they escaped by poking his one eye out, as shown in this vase decoration (above).

When the queen of Crete gave birth to the Minotaur the horrified king imprisoned it in the centre of a vast maze. Theseus entered and fought the Minotaur (left). He secretly unrolled thread as he went through the maze. This marked the paths he had already taken, so that he did not wander around the maze for ever.

The Greek sphinx, unlike that of the ancient Egyptians, was female. She had the head of a woman, the body of a lion and the wings of a bird. She preyed on passers-by in the Theban hills, asking riddles and eating those who answered incorrectly.

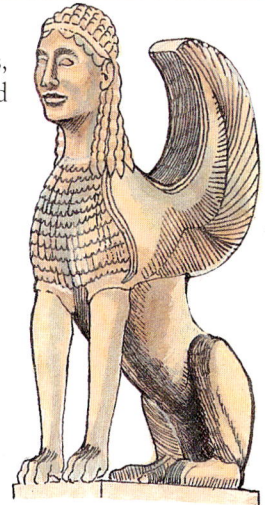

These are centaurs (above) – human to the waist and horse below – battling with a lion. Most centaurs were lawless creatures who were uncontrollable if given wine. A few centaurs were noble and gentle. Chiron, the wisest of all, was a foster parent to many heroes.

The creature pictured left is a griffin, taken from a bronze relief of c. 650 BC. It has the body of a lion, the head of an eagle and powerful wings.

Left, a scene from a terracotta relief c. 475 BC. The hero Bellerophon is fighting the Chimera. The chimera had two heads (a lion's and a goat's), its tail was a serpent and it breathed fire.

The gorgon Medusa (shown above) was so terrifying that anyone caught in her gaze was turned to stone. Her hair was a mass of snakes, she had wings of gold and claws of bronze. The hero Perseus managed to kill her without looking into her deadly eyes. He looked at her reflection in his shield instead.

The Cloud-Eater

A legend from the Zuni people of New Mexico

The Cloud-Eater had an enormous mouth and an endless appetite for clouds. Every day he stood on the mountain peak with his mouth wide open and swallowed every cloud that came along. Not one escaped him, so no rain fell upon the land. People could no longer grow their crops and began to starve.

"We must kill Cloud-Eater," they said. But no one was brave enough to try. A young boy called Ahaiyuta heard his grandmother lamenting about Cloud-Eater. "I shall go to the mountain and kill him," he told her. "If you must go," said his grandmother, "take these four feathers. The red feather will show you the way. The blue feather will let you talk with animals. The yellow feather will make you as small as you wish and the black feather will give you the strength you need."

Ahaiyuta put the red feather in his hair, tucked the others in his belt and set off. As he went along he noticed a gopher sitting outside its hole. He thrust the blue and the yellow feathers into his hair, so that when the gopher called him into its burrow he understood and could slip in easily. The gopher's tunnel led deep inside the mountain, so close to the giant that they could hear him snoring as he slept.

"This is the place," said the gopher and it gnawed through the earth to make a tunnel to the monster's chest. Ahaiyuta put the black feather in his hair, took aim, and sent his arrow speeding down the tunnel, straight into the monster's heart.

The Cloud-Eater gave a roar that shook the mountain and then was silent for ever. When the clouds gathered, rain fell on the land once again.

Mythical birds

The Simurgh is pictured below on a Persian dish of the 7th–8th century.

Many legendary birds are noble and helpful. Persia is the home of the Simurgh. The Simurgh rescued the baby Prince Zal from the mountains where he had been left to die by his father who thought his unnaturally white hair was a sign of evil. The Simurgh cared for the baby in her nest with her own young. When he was old enough to go out into the world, she gave him one of her feathers, telling him to light it in times of peril. Zal first lit the feather years later, when he feared his young wife was dying in childbirth. The sky darkened and the Simurgh appeared. She told him that his was no ordinary child. After the prince's baby boy had been born the Simurgh healed the mother with special potions. The boy was named Rustam and the Simurgh predicted that he would grow up to become his nation's greatest hero.

The phoenix (right), fabled to live in Arabia, was the only one of its kind and had no mate. Every five hundred years it would build itself a funeral pyre and leap into the flames. From its ashes a new phoenix would arise.

The North American Thunderbird (left) brings storms and rain and its eyes flash lightning.

Slaying a dragon

Dragons show up in myths and legends around the world. In China, the majority of dragons are portrayed as good and kind creatures, but elsewhere it is generally agreed that dragons are bad things and it is a hero's job to slay them. This is never an easy task, as the Norse thunder god Thor discovered when he tried to kill Jormundgand, the World Serpent.

This long and snake-like dragon lived in the ocean, its body encircling the world. Hot-headed Thor decided to hunt it. He persuaded Hymir the giant to take him fishing. Thor rowed so hard that he soon had the boat out in the middle of the ocean. Hymir began to tremble, though he was many times the size of Thor, and begged him to turn back. But Thor baited his line with an ox's head and cast it into the water. In the depths, the serpent saw the morsel and gulped it down. The sea rolled and boiled as he thrashed about, but Thor heaved so hard that he pulled the monster's head right out of the water. This was too much for Hymir. He grabbed a sharp knife and hacked Thor's fishing line in two. The serpent escaped and Thor kicked Hymir into the sea in fury.

Some myths of ancient Babylon tell of a she-dragon formed from the salt waters that existed before the world was made. Her name was Tiamat. She and her husband Apsu were the parents of the first gods, whose descendants began to quarrel. One group killed Apsu and another provoked Tiamat into avenging him.

Tiamat created an army of serpent-demons and scorpion-men and led them into battle with the hostile gods. The gods were so horrified at the sight of this army that none of their leaders dared to face it. Even Ea, wisest of them all, was in despair. Only Marduk, the son of Ea, was willing to fight. But before he set off he made the gods swear to obey him as their king forever if he won. Marduk mounted his storm chariot and armed himself with lightning. He took a net, held at the corners by the four winds, and rode to meet Tiamat. He flung the net over her and forced her throat open with a hurricane which raged and swelled inside her. Then with an arrow he split her heart and cut her body in two. He lifted one half up to form the sky and from the other half he made the Earth. This is how the world began and how Marduk became ruler of all things.

The Persian hero Rustam travelled through Mazdaran, a land full of demons, upon his magnificent horse, Rakhsh. A dragon approached while Rustam slept. Rakhsh pawed the ground to wake his master but the dragon vanished before he opened his eyes. It played this game repeatedly until Rustam grew furious and threatened to cut off his horse's head if it did not let him sleep. At the dragon's next appearance the brave horse attacked it. Rustam heard the monster's roar just in time to behead it and save the faithful Rakhsh from its jaws (left).

Miscellaneous myths

A **rain myth from the Fon people of West Africa:**
When the great goddess Mawu made the universe, she told her two sons, Sagbata and Sogbo, to rule it together. This went well for a time but before long they began to quarrel. Finally, Sagbata the elder brother declared he could not put up with Sogbo's interference any longer. He declared that he would take all his mother's wealth and go down to the Earth to live.

Sagbata collected all his mother's possessions and put them in a large bag. As he did so he thought, 'I had better not include water in the bag or it will make everything wet. I shall have to leave it behind'. When his packing was finished he descended to Earth. It was so difficult that he realised he would never be able to climb back again.

Up in the sky Sogbo saw his chance to gain complete power. "I will see that no more rain falls on the Earth" he said. "Let's see what Sagbata can do about that!" Soon the plants throughout the world began to shrivel and the rivers dried up.
"Send us rain!" the people cried to Sagbata. But Sagbata had no water to make rain.
"Do not worry," he told them. "It will rain soon."

But months passed, then years and still no rain fell. Sagbata realised he would have to make it up with his brother. He sent a message offering Sagbata the rule of the Earth as well as the sky, if only he would send rain.

Up in the sky Sogbo smiled. "When my brother took our mother's wealth he was unwise to leave water behind. Whoever controls water controls the universe."

Then, with a rumble of thunder, he sent rain to the thirsty Earth and everyone praised Sogbo, great god of the Earth and sky.

A **moon myth from the Urubu people of the Amazon:**
Long ago the sky was always completely black at night because there was no moon.

One day a great feast was held to celebrate the arrival of a new baby. Its parents invited all their friends and relations to help choose a name for the child. By sunset people were still arguing about the new name and nothing had been decided. A young couple became bored. The woman persuaded the man that she could help him to create a surprise for the party. She took him into a hut and painted his face. She put black circles round his eyes, a thick black line down his nose and black all round his mouth.

The man was sure she was trying to make him look ridiculous and told her to wash the black off. But no matter how much he rubbed at his face the marks would not disappear. When everyone else saw him they shouted with laughter.
"A man looking like that doesn't have enough sense to choose a name," they said, and chased him from the feast.

The man was ashamed and very angry. He picked up his bow and shot an arrow into the air, sending it so high that it stuck in the sky. He shot a second arrow that pierced the end of the first, then another and another, until a ladder of arrows hung from the sky. Then he climbed up them to escape the laughter and hid in the sky. The woman who had caused all the trouble went up after him and they were never seen again.

Three nights later, a light appeared in the sky. It was the crescent moon and each night it grew a little larger until it showed its full face. People could see dark marks upon it just like those on the face of the man who had disappeared into the darkness.
"There is our brother in the sky!" people cried. "And that bright star that follows him each night must be our sister, still trying to wash the marks from his face."

*A*n Indian myth about death:

Yama, the god of death, reigned over Yamapur, the underworld. He was a grim but fair ruler and was not cruel. Yama wasn't popular with the other gods because he caused such fear and sorrow in the living. To make up for this Yama married many wives and always had friendly company in the underworld. But once he fell in love with a mortal woman. He disguised himself as a mortal man and won her hand only to discover that he had made a terrible mistake. His new wife had a hideous temper. She made his days miserable with her jealousy and spite, so that before long he retreated and hid in the underworld.

Not long after this, Yama's mortal wife bore him a son who grew up to be a fine boy. Yama proudly kept an eye on him from a distance. When the boy reached manhood his father taught him the use of herbs to cure diseases and he became a doctor. He soon became famous for his skills and always knew whether he could cure a sickness or whether it was beyond his abilities. The truth was, Yama gave him help. If his father appeared to him at a bedside and nodded, the patient would recover; if he shook his head, there was no hope and the person would inevitably follow Yama into the underworld.

One day Yama's son was called to attend a princess whom many doctors had failed to cure. Yama appeared by her bed and shook his head. But the princess was so beautiful that his son refused to accept his father's decision. "Do not take her!" he begged. "Let her live a few years longer." "Three days, and no more," said Yama. "I will grant you that because you are my son."

After three days the young man was completely in love with the princess. When Yama arrived to carry her off, his son tried to argue once more, but the god of death would not relent. "If you take her," said his son, "I will tell my mother where you are and how to find you." Yama trembled with dread and granted him the life of the princess. Her grateful parents then allowed the young doctor to take her as his bride.

A Slav myth about household gods:

When the Great God created heaven and Earth, he drove the rebellious spirits out of the sky and they tumbled down to Earth. They fell onto the roofs of houses, into farmyards, fields and wild places – marshes, rivers and forests. Wherever they fell they made themselves at home. The gods who landed in the wild places remained just as wicked as ever and it was wise for humans to keep out of their way. But those who lived close to people grew more friendly, though they could still be tricky to deal with.

Every house had its own little god, whose name was the Domovoi. The Domovoi was usually a hairy little man – he even had hair on the palms of his hands. Some people said they had glimpsed a tail and horns on him and in some households he would look like one of the farm animals or even a pile of hay. If the Domovoi remained in a good mood he brought his house good luck. He wept if there was going to be a death in the family and pulled the wife's hair to warn her if her husband was going to beat her. When a family moved to a new house the Domovoi moved too – the housewife had to cut a slice of bread and put it under the stove to welcome him in.

The Domovoi was not the only god of the house because he had a wife who lived in the cellar. She was called the Kikimora. She helped with the housework, but only if the housewife was hardworking too. If she was lazy the Kikimora played all kinds of tricks and tickled the children at night to make them cry.

Glossary

Aboriginal The first people known to inhabit a land although it is usually used to refer specifically to the first people of Australia.

Anglo Saxon The people or belonging to the people of England before the Norman Conquest.

Arabia The vast, largely desert peninsula separated from Africa by the Red Sea.

Aztecs The dominant people of central Mexico in the 16th century.

Babylon The capital of the Babylonian empire which flourished in Mesopotamia (modern Iraq) from about 1900-100 BC and again, after Assyrian domination, from 626-539 BC.

Celts People living in central and western Europe in ancient Greek and Roman times. Except in western parts of Britain and France, their culture was destroyed by the Romans and by invaders from northern Europe.

Classical world A name given to the civilisation of the ancient Greeks and Romans.

Gopher A small burrowing rodent of North and Central America.

Haida A Native American tribe of the North Pacific coast of America.

Hittites The people of an empire that flourished in Anatolia (in modern Turkey) between c 1750-1200 BC.

Llama A South American relative of the camel. Llama wool can be used for making clothes.

Lodge A Native American tent or house.

Lyre An ancient Greek stringed instrument like a small harp.

Mandans A Native American people of the Upper Missouri River valley.

Maze A complicated arrangement of passageways opening into each other. They have many dead ends and are designed so that it is easy to get lost.

Mortal All living things are mortal and will eventually die.

Mummy A dead body preserved from decay by being dried, filled with spices and wrapped in bandages.

Nez Perce A Native American people of a region of northwestern USA.

Norse Relating to the Germanic peoples (the ancestors of the Germans, Scandinavians and English). The myths are called Norse because the earliest written versions of them are in Norwegian.

Oracle A sacred place where a god was believed to answer people's questions, usually through the mouth of a priest or priestess who spoke in a trance.

Polynesian Belonging to a group of widely scattered islands in the central South Pacific ocean.

Pyre A pile of wood on which a dead body is burned.

Quetzal A bird that lives in central America.

Quiver A case for holding arrows.

Red Branch The name of the band of warriors serving King Conor of Ulster.

Sioux A group of related tribes from the plains of central North America.

Slavs A group of peoples who came from Asia into Eastern Europe in ancient times. Their descendants can now be found in Russia, Poland and other countries of central and eastern Europe.

Tinglit A Native American tribe of the North Pacific coast of America.

Titans The first race of Greek gods, who were defeated by Zeus, ruler of the Olympian gods (so-called because they lived on Mount Olympus).

Vishnu One of the greatest gods of the Hindu religion.

Index

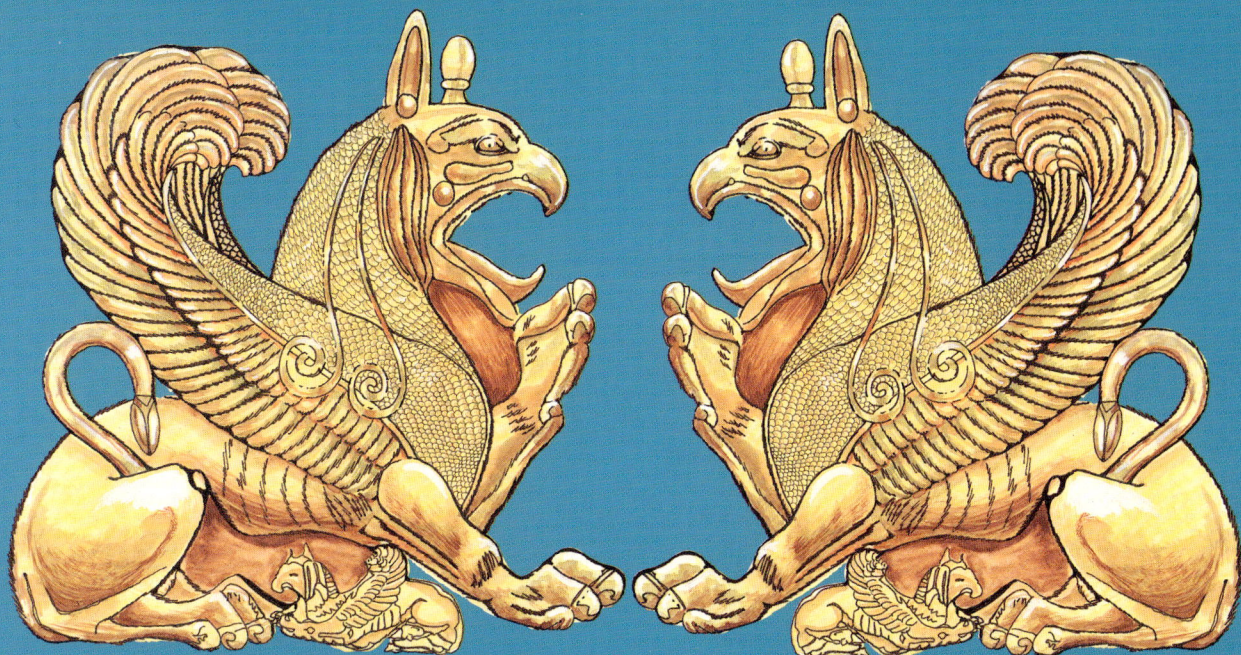

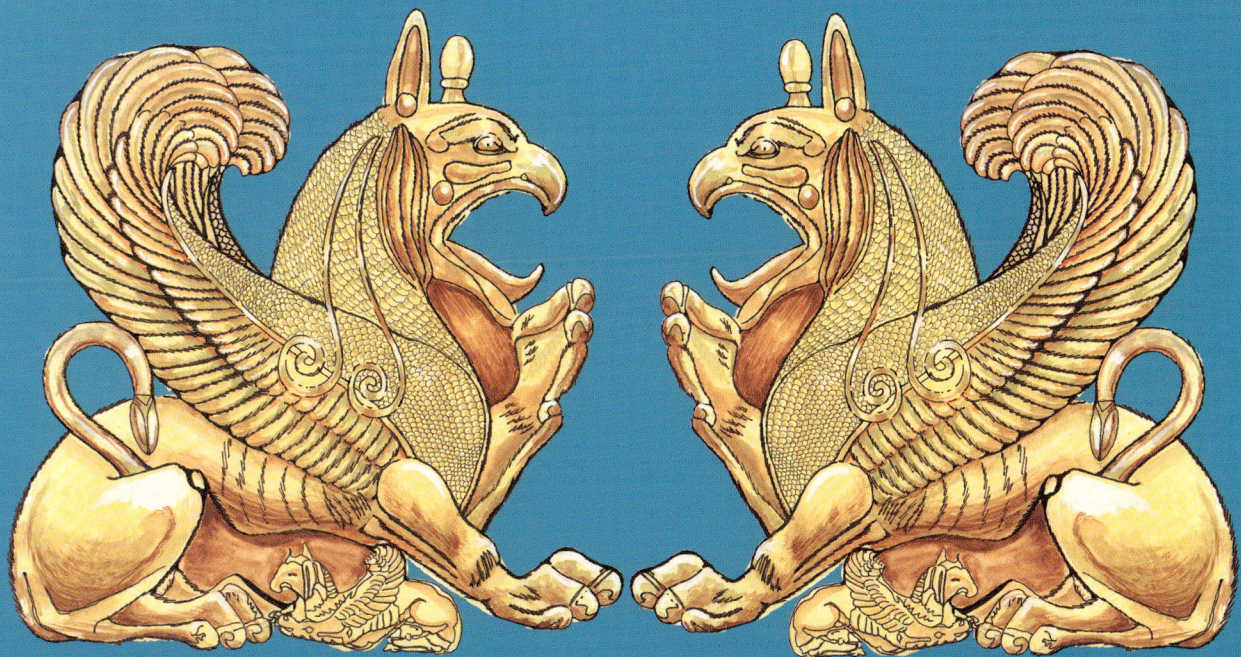